Sandra Bullock

Lucent Books, San Diego, CA

Titles in the People in the News series include:

Garth Brooks
Sandra Bullock
George W. Bush
Jim Carrey
Tom Cruise
Bill Gates
John Grisham
Jesse Jackson
Michael Jackson
Michael Jordan
Stephen King
George Lucas
Dominique Moceanu
Rosie O'Donnell
Colin Powell
Princess Diana
Christopher Reeve
The Rolling Stones
Steven Spielberg
R. L. Stine
Jesse Ventura
Oprah Winfrey
Tiger Woods

PEOPLE
IN THE NEWS

Sandra Bullock

by Anne E. Hill

Lucent Books, San Diego, CA

For my husband, George: Here's to the years ahead.

Library of Congress Cataloging-in-Publication Data

Hill, Anne E.
  Sandra Bullock / by Anne E. Hill
    p. cm. — (People in the news)
  Includes bibliographical references and index.
  ISBN 1-56006-711-X (alk. paper)
  1. Bullock, Sandra—Juvenile literature. 2. Motion picture actors and actresses—United States—Biography—Juvenile literature.
  [1. Bullock, Sandra. 2. Actors and actresses. 3. Women—Biography.]
  I. Title. II. People in the news (San Diego, Calif.)
  PN2287.B737 H55   2001
  791.43'028'092—dc21

                                                          00–009367

Table of Contents

Foreword

FAME AND CELEBRITY are alluring. People are drawn to those who walk in fame's spotlight, whether they are known for great accomplishments or for notorious deeds. The lives of the famous pique public interest and attract attention, perhaps because their experiences seem in some ways so different from, yet in other ways so similar to, our own.

Newspapers, magazines, and television regularly capitalize on this fascination with celebrity by running profiles of famous people. For example, television programs such as *Entertainment Tonight* devote all of their programming to stories about entertainment and entertainers. Magazines such as *People* fill their pages with stories of the private lives of famous people. Even newspapers, newsmagazines, and television news frequently delve into the lives of well-known personalities. Despite the number of articles and programs, few provide more than a superficial glimpse at their subjects.

Lucent's People in the News series offers young readers a deeper look into the lives of today's newsmakers, the influences that have shaped them, and the impact they have had in their fields of endeavor and on other people's lives. The subjects of the series hail from many disciplines and walks of life. They include authors, musicians, athletes, political leaders, entertainers, entrepreneurs, and others who have made a mark on modern life and who, in many cases, will continue to do so for years to come.

These biographies are more than factual chronicles. Each book emphasizes the contributions, accomplishments, or deeds that have brought fame or notoriety to the individual and shows how that person has influenced modern life. Authors portray their subjects in a realistic, unsentimental light. For example, Bill Gates—the cofounder and chief executive officer of the

6

software giant Microsoft—has been instrumental in making personal computers the most vital tool of the modern age. Few dispute his business savvy, his perseverance, or his technical expertise, yet critics say he is ruthless in his dealings with competitors and driven more by his desire to maintain Microsoft's dominance in the computer industry than by an interest in furthering technology.

In these books, young readers will encounter inspiring stories about real people who achieved success despite enormous obstacles. Oprah Winfrey—the most powerful, most watched, and wealthiest woman on television today—spent the first six years of her life in the care of her grandparents while her unwed mother sought work and a better life elsewhere. Her adolescence was colored by promiscuity, pregnancy at age fourteen, rape, and sexual abuse.

Each author documents and supports his or her work with an array of primary and secondary source quotations taken from diaries, letters, speeches, and interviews. All quotes are footnoted to show readers exactly how and where biographers derive their information and provide guidance for further research. The quotations enliven the text by giving readers eyewitness views of the life and accomplishments of each person covered in the People in the News series.

In addition, each book in the series includes photographs, annotated bibliographies, timelines, and comprehensive indexes. For both the casual reader and the student researcher, the People in the News series offers insight into the lives of today's newsmakers—people who shape the way we live, work, and play in the modern age.

Introduction

"The Girl Next Door"

Every generation of film stars has a wholesome sweetheart who lights up the screen, making her irresistible to audiences. In their time, actresses such as Sally Field, Doris Day, and Sandra Dee all held the title of the squeaky-clean girl next door. Sandra Bullock is considered the girl next door for the new millennium. Even at the young age of eighteen, students at her high school in Virginia recognized Bullock's comedic appeal, voting her "Class Clown." Years later, having charmed audiences in films such as *Speed, While You Were Sleeping,* and *Hope Floats,* the thirty-five-year-old actress is loved for her wholesome familiarity. But she is much more than she appears on-screen.

Although that wholesome image usually translates into certain box office success, Bullock instead seeks out roles that allow her to grow as both a person and an actor. For her role in the 2000 film *28 Days,* in which she plays a recovering alcoholic, she even voluntarily checked herself into an alcohol rehabilitation center.

Bullock's style has helped broaden the image of the Hollywood actress from a sexy, aloof, and shallow seductress to an accessible, fun-loving, emotionally complex woman. Her down-to-earth attitude has won her praise from costars and fans. She has no desire to come off as superior and would rather just hang out and talk. "I'm not what the industry or the media have deemed a hot tamale," she said in 1995. "There is something comfortable about me. I'm like a sleeper sofa. A good couch your grandmother has."[1]

Magazines like *Entertainment Weekly* say she is the woman most girls want to be like and the one most men want to date.

Fans adore Sandra Bullock's wholesome, girl-next-door appeal.

"Men treat me like someone they're comfortable with, talking guy talk. I'm a good ear for men and a good voice for the women's side,"[2] Bullock explained.

With her reported asking price at more than $12 million a film, Bullock could simply continue playing the girl next door that audiences expect. She prefers, however, not to get typecast.

Her role in 1996's *A Time to Kill* was the first of many casting departures. She played a mouthy, ambitious law student who helps defend a black man accused of shooting two white men who raped and tortured his ten-year-old daughter. Bullock got some good reviews for the role and has gone on to portray many other types of characters, including an early-twentieth-century nurse in *In Love and War* and a wild, free spirit in *Forces of Nature*.

But, as evidenced by the large box office receipts for her romantic comedies, fans are still happiest when Bullock plays the sweetheart. The actress is aware of the dilemma but unwilling to give in to it. "Everyone wants me to get stuck in sweet parts," Bullock says. "There is a whole other side of me that wants to get out."[3]

Chapter 1

Fitting In and Standing Out

SANDRA ANNETTE BULLOCK was born on July 26, 1964, in Washington, D.C., the first child of John and Helga Bullock. From the start, Sandra's life was unique, thanks to the background of her parents. John Bullock was a young man from a large Irish-English family in Alabama. He had worked his way through Juilliard, a prestigious performing arts school in New York, and had a job as a civilian for the Pentagon in Nuremberg, Germany.

There, he met Helga Meyer, twelve years his junior. The daughter of a German rocket engineer, Helga was clerking in Nuremberg to support her voice studies at a music conservatory. "It's one of those great stories: she would bicycle her way to work and he'd drive the Mercedes by her. And she was the fledgling opera singer, and he didn't know it, and she didn't know he was into opera,"[4] Bullock relayed to a reporter at *British Premiere* magazine.

A Transatlantic Life

Helga and John soon connected over their love for opera, and their interest in one another grew. They married and began a transcontinental life together, living outside Washington, D.C., and other cities in the United States depending on John's work. They returned to Europe every year for the opera season, during which Helga performed. In addition to his office work as an administrator at the Pentagon, John also gave voice lessons.

Because her father never had a boy, Sandra jokes that she was raised as the son. She was rambunctious and tomboyish, while her

11

sister Gesine (four-and-a-half years her junior) was more feminine.
"I was very much a tomboy at a very young age," Sandra admits,
"just because most of the kids in the neighborhood were boys, and
that seemed like the only way you're going to get to be able to
play [with them]."[5] She preferred to roughhouse with the boys
rather than play quietly with her sister.

Although she and Gesine, who is now a lawyer, are very
close today, Sandra admits that she wasn't the greatest big sister
when they were young. Like most siblings, the two fought over
everything from toys to rules to gaining the attention of their
parents. In fact, Sandra admits that her first ambition was to kill
Gesine because she was jealous of all the attention lavished on
the little girl. She would pinch her sister hard enough to make
her cry and even admits to chasing her around with scissors on
one occasion.

Sandra's experience with sibling rivalry was not uncommon,
but being raised in two countries was. When in Germany, she
stayed in Nuremberg with her great aunt and grandmother, and
she is fluent in their native German. Today, she credits her
transatlantic upbringing with her ability to adapt to new situa-
tions. She told *McCall's StarStyle*,

> I always said I never want to be someone who's at a
> party where I feel I don't belong. I want to to be able to
> fit in and make the best of it, wherever. I want to feel I
> can add something, shift to another part of my heritage,
> my background, my childhood, my philosophies, and
> add something to the conversation.[6]

When the family wasn't traveling, Sandra would pal around
and build things with her father on the weekends. She enjoyed
her dad's company, perhaps even more than her mom's. "My
dad is pretty much a jokester . . . and I think I was more a
daddy's girl in my formative years. So I spent a lot of time chasing after him and doing as he did,"[7] Sandra explained. The two
even made the carved canopy bed that Sandra slept in as a child.

In the evenings and on weekends, Sandra would listen to her
parents sing. Today, she's a fan of the opera music they loved,

Sandra Bullock with her father, John. As a child, Bullock especially enjoyed spending time with her "jokester" father.

but she admits that when she was young, she did not enjoy it. Sandra thought it was too loud and was sometimes embarrassed when kids in the neighborhood complained about the noise. "My sister and I would think, Please can you tone it down a little? We wanted them banned to the closet."[8]

Sandra now appreciates her opera background and claims she can identify an aria from just about any opera. She has fun humming a few bars and nonchalantly telling whoever is with her the name of the piece and the composer. In fact, it was through opera that Sandra got her first opportunity to perform.

A Taste for Performing

When she was eight years old, Sandra played a gypsy child in the background of one of her mother's productions in Salzburg, Austria. Although she did not sing or speak, the audiences threw her chocolates by way of applause. She loved the feeling of performing, the hustle and bustle backstage, and she loved the chocolate.

Following that success, Sandra had several more opportunities to perform. She enjoyed making a little money for her appearances and eventually sang in the chorus of an opera. She describes the atmosphere as very flamboyant and loud, which she loved. The backstage area was full of activity. Performers rushed around putting on their makeup, getting dressed, talking, and practicing their singing. The little girl especially enjoyed goofing off during rehearsals and making the other performers laugh. She was rambunctious and had a gift for comedy even at a young age.

Theater, and a flair for the dramatic, was in Sandra's blood. It was during her opera experiences that she knew she had found her calling. "I want to be an actor because you get to sing, dance and meet people from different countries,"[9] she wrote in a diary that her mother recently discovered. Sandra announced her intentions to her parents, who were more than happy with her career choice. They did what they could to nurture the performer in their young daughter.

When she was nine years old, Sandra made her first movie with a video camera and her neighbors as cast and crew. Years later, her mother unearthed that footage, and Sandra told a reporter what she remembered from her first original production:

> I cast it, did the wardrobe, I got all my neighbors to partake in the production. I'd set up the camera. And apparently . . . I was wearing a blonde wig and I had stuffed myself to the nines in the front and the behind. My mother said I had huge boobs and a huge butt, and this purple glittery outfit on. I was a secretary of some sort. At some point there was a toilet flushing, which I thought was hysterical.[10]

Besides a sense of humor, Sandra had ambition. She knew, however, that her ambition would separate her from all the other kids. Her mother was a performer and was very different from the other mothers. For one thing, she dressed like a performer. "I remember I was in second grade," Sandra recalls, "and I hear the click of my mother's shoes coming down the hallway, and I thought, Oh no. . . . She was a very hippie chick, in pigtails and little bangly shoes. . . . But I wanted her to be normal—to wear perfect clothes like all the other mothers."[11]

Rather than stand out like her mother, Sandra chose to repress her instincts for the sake of fitting in with her peers. She expressed her theatrical side on the stage in the cosmopolitan cities in Europe, where her talents made her special in a good way, rather than a negative one. While in America, however, she tried to live a regular, suburban existence.

The one type of performing she did allow herself to be involved in in the United States was her father's voice lessons. As a spectator, Sandra met many famous people, including actor Anthony Quinn, whom John taught to use his voice onstage in

Actor Anthony Quinn, one of John Bullock's voice students.

Zorba. Rock musicians also appeared at the Bullock home to be retrained in the vocal basics. Sandra enjoyed watching the vocalists work with her father, and she developed a large amount of respect for her father's abilities. This, coupled with her spending much of her free time with her father, made their relationship very strong.

A Close Call

The close relationship Sandra shared with her father almost ended when she was still a child. When she was ten, a bulldozer crushed her father on their Virginia property. He lay there for twenty-four hours, waiting to be found. The event was life altering for Sandra and her family. She said,

> I felt like I was the man of the house in a very weird way, because I got the phone call. I had to relay it to my mother. My dad was in the hospital for a year. They wanted to amputate his legs, but my mom was, "No, I will not have it," and after the seventh doctor they found a young guy who was amazing. My father had been a tower of strength to us, and even all through his hospital stay, he'd know we were coming so he'd have the nurses set up a bottle of vodka or whatever on the IV and he'd pretend he was drunk. Now, he's got scars and he can't go jogging, but he's back to normal—as normal as you can get when you've been run over by a bulldozer—and does all the things he did before. It sort of made me fearful. It sort of established that people went away, so I never really allowed myself to get close to people that I really love, or I never let myself show it. Because if I showed it, all of a sudden something's going to happen. And you get over that in time, but I know it molded my personality.[12]

Young Sandra's sense of security was rattled, and the experience made her fearful of death. After John's near-death experience, the Bullocks tried to sell the property, but there were no interested buyers. So, the family stayed on in Virginia.

Childhood Scars

Unlike the emotional scars left by her father's brush with death, most of Bullock's scars are easy to see. She had her share of emergency room traumas as a kid. Before her father's injury, Sandra cracked her head open at their same mountain property, and when she was eleven, she fell into a creek near her house and got a small scar over her right eye. Today, many people think she had cosmetic surgery on her nose, but she hasn't. "The truth is, my sister Gesine broke it. She was raising the garage door and her elbow cracked me right on the nose. I've been stuck with it ever since," Bullock told *People* magazine, in the May 10, 1999, issue. Although she once thought her nose and scar made her less attractive, these traits eventually gave Sandra her distinctive appearance. She has long since forgiven her sister.

Fitting In

By the time she was twelve, the Bullock family was in permanent residence in Arlington, Virginia. Sandra temporarily put her aspirations of being an actress on hold while she studied and struggled to fit in at her new junior high school. She looked different and had trouble relating to her classmates, who seemed to prefer socializing to studying.

Sandra was flat-chested, wore glasses, and was not fashionable like many of the girls in the affluent, suburban neighborhood. "I wore green bell bottoms and I had a big bowl-shaped haircut. The word 'dog' was used a lot,"[13] she remembered.

Instead of reacting negatively, Sandra relied on a good sense of humor to deal with the teasing. Years later, happy and successful as an actress, she revealed that the sense of humor she cultivated in childhood had served her well. It made her develop a side to her personality that shines in comedic roles. In fact, as Sandra says, her humor often gets her and those around her through difficult times:

> There's one thing that puts people at ease and that's humor. I'd say 50 percent of my humor is because I feel great and the other 50 percent is because I want to make others feel comfortable, so I can get comfortable. It's definitely a control zone. You look at the funniest person in

show business, and I'll show you someone who's been through a lot of garbage.[14]

Growing Up

In addition to looking different, Sandra also struggled with her schoolwork. In elementary school, she had been a straight-A student. "The only way I could conform . . . was not to be smart," Sandra revealed. "I did well in classes until I realized that it was another thing against me, then my grades were horrible."[15]

Helga Bullock didn't understand her daughter's need to fit in and look like the other kids in her class. Helga had always taught her children to be unique and strong-willed individuals. As Sandra brooded over fitting in, locked her diary, and acted differently around her parents, Helga worried that her daughter was using drugs. Luckily, her fears proved ungrounded. Sandra was just in the midst of reinventing herself—and discovering boys.

Around this time, Sandra had her first boyfriend. "He asked me to go steady with him," she remembered. "Then a friend had a party where our parents dropped us off. We sat on a couch, and I think I kissed him for about an hour; your lips are numb but you don't stop."[16]

Although their relationship didn't last long, Sandra made a decision: She wanted boys to like her; she wanted to fit in and be popular. "I got a job cleaning in this insurance company and worked after school to earn money so I could buy clothes. I decided, OK, I will conform,"[17] Sandra said.

Looking back, she concludes that her decision made her happier then, but depressed now. She learned that fitting in and being miserable wasn't as rewarding as standing out and doing what she loved. "I became incredibly ordinary," she says. "Everything I owned was monogrammed."[18]

The teenager even decided to concentrate on gymnastics and cheerleading to fit in with the popular kids. She dressed like everyone else, participated in "normal" after-school activities, and did just enough to get by in the classroom. As a result, Sandra was accepted into the "in crowd." She says, "Everybody who had never spoken to me was suddenly a really good friend of mine. It was sad."[19]

High School Days

In 1978, fourteen-year-old Sandra enrolled at Washington-Lee High School in Arlington. She spent her time cheerleading, hanging out with friends, and dating a football player. In all her attempts to fit in, however, she didn't give up her sense of humor. "She could make anyone laugh," one classmate recalled. "She wasn't smoking or wearing ripped clothes. She didn't do drugs. She was an above-average student, but no brainiac."[20] Sandra's popularity would result in her being named "Class Clown" by her 1982 senior class.

Still, while her popular friends thought she was happy to be one of them, her teachers saw another side to her personality. Gerrie Filpi, her high school drama teacher, remembered that Sandra paid a price for her popularity. Filpi saw a quick wit and tremendous intellectual ability beneath Sandy's cool and flippant facade. "Sandra was so popular," Filpi says, "there was so much attention paid to her, that she didn't spend as much time as she should evolving."[21]

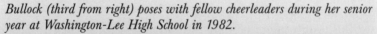

Bullock (third from right) poses with fellow cheerleaders during her senior year at Washington-Lee High School in 1982.

But that would soon change. At seventeen, Sandra finally outgrew her need to fit in. As graduation day neared, she decided that she was through conforming and was ready to make her own decisions and pursue her dream of drama. Because her father had attended a prestigious performing arts school, her parents wanted her to go to Juilliard. They had high hopes for their oldest daughter. But although Sandra wanted to act, she also wanted to be surrounded by different types of people, from different backgrounds, studying different subjects. "I wanted to go to a school where you could meet people, have a boyfriend," Sandra says. "Where they have fraternities. I wanted to grow up and I wanted to grow up in a normal school."[22]

She found that environment at East Carolina University in Greenville, North Carolina. It wasn't too far from home, but it was still a major move. ECU offered many subjects, including theater, and had many different organizations and activities. Many students from her high school attended ECU and Sandra liked the campus. Although she had traveled the world, the teen had never been away from her family. As she packed her bags and chose her courses, eighteen-year-old Sandra felt truly nervous for the first time in her young life.

Chapter 2

Bit Parts

An EXCITED AND nervous Sandra Bullock became a college freshman in the fall of 1982. Although she admits to being naive and "green," as she calls herself, she was determined to make the best of her college years. One of the first things she did when she arrived at the campus was locate the theater department and sign up for as many drama courses as she could.

Stage Time

At first, Bullock was determined to make her mark as a comedic actress in campus productions. However, her acting teacher, Don Biehn, saw a serious side to her. When Biehn approached her about trying her hand at drama, Bullock was apprehensive but eventually gave it a try. "I was so young and intimidated, and here came a teacher who brought New York to me. And if it wasn't for him, I wouldn't have had the discipline,"[23] she says.

Biehn and other professors helped encourage Bullock's talent. "They were just so good at seeing someone who was insecure and needed nurturing,"[24] Bullock recalls. That nurturing made Bullock comfortable. She took chances onstage and revealed more vulnerable parts of herself, instead of always hiding behind a mask of comedy.

With her raw talent and teachers' help, Bullock auditioned for, and won, a role in the campus production of Anton Chekhov's *Three Sisters*. The role as one of three sisters who loses everything she loves, including her father's estate, was a demanding one. "It's a highly charged piece, and she was trying to give the emotional moment in every scene, trying to hit a home run," Biehn said. "I remember thinking, 'She is fearless.'"[25]

Biehn was right; Bullock admits she didn't know fear because she hadn't yet experienced professional failure. At ECU, her grades were good, she was getting the opportunity to act, and she had a good group of friends. But it wasn't enough for Bullock. ECU was a long way from the bright lights of New York City, which were calling her.

Getting Restless

With each year that passed, Bullock grew more and more restless in the small town of Greenville. No longer content there, she considered transferring to NYU or Juilliard in order to be closer to the acting opportunities in Manhattan. The decision she made to attend ECU as a seventeen-year-old high school senior no longer fit in with her more ambitious twenty-one-year-old mind-set. Finally, in her senior year, just three credits shy of graduating, Bullock decided to leave North Carolina for New York City. Bullock explains,

> I had things to do. I just wanted to go and do theater and work in New York. I packed up the car and went. That was the ultimate. I went knowing one person, and I was kind of glad because you could start from scratch. You didn't have the cliques you had in school, where everyone knew the best one in class – the one who could cry the best, the one who did Shakespeare the best. And I wanted to be the best comedian. I wanted to be the female Jerry Lewis.[26]

Bullock's parents were unhappy with their daughter's decision not to finish college, but they also understood her desire to perform. When she looks back at her unfinished college career, Bullock thinks her missed diploma was thanks in part only "to some psychology class that I probably should have taken."[27]

The Big Apple

Although technically an adult, Bullock was like a child when she arrived in the expensive city of New York, optimistic but penniless. Luckily, her father kept a small apartment in the city for the

Eager to immerse herself in acting, Bullock moved to New York City in 1986.

vocal lessons he taught there and he let her move in. Bullock still needed to make money, however. She soon discovered that many aspiring actors and actresses took jobs as waiters or bartenders at night in order to be available for auditions and lessons during the day. Bullock, however, had no experience in the restaurant or bar business. She admits to fibbing her way into a bartender's job. "I didn't know how to mix any fancy drinks. The customers helped me," [28] she later told *People* magazine.

Though she struggled with customers' orders at night, during the day Bullock studied Method acting with Sanford Meisner at the renowned Neighborhood Playhouse. In the Method style of acting, actors strive for close personal identification with the characters they are portraying. Like her college drama professors, Meisner saw ability in her. He also knew that even with her talent, she needed to pay her dues, and he urged her to get her feet wet.

So, Bullock began a seemingly endless round of auditions. Desperate to expand her résumé, as well as pay the bills, she took parts in student films for $25 a day. "You'd have to go out to New Jersey and bring your own clothes and make-up and act horribly,"[29] she recalled. Still, she was determined to make it in New York.

Off-Broadway

In 1988, twenty-three-year-old Sandra Bullock thought she had found her big break when she was cast in the off-Broadway play *No Time Flat.* Though she hoped it would lead to bigger and better parts, the play was panned by critics and soon closed. What appeared to be a failure, however, actually helped her career.

New York magazine critic John Simon praised Bullock's performance in the show, and she used the review to help land an agent. Soon she was receiving advanced word of open auditions and even getting calls to meet with directors. Bullock still couldn't quit her night job but hoped her situation would soon improve. She knew if it didn't, she'd have to let go of her dream, because she was running low on funds. "There was only one time when I said I was going to quit this business, in my early

Method Acting

Method acting is perhaps the most popular acting style for contemporary performers. Used by both stage and screen actors, the Method was founded by Russian Konstantin Stanislavski, director of the Moscow Art Theater and author of a number of books on acting in the late nineteenth and early twentieth centuries.

The Method requires a performer to draw on his or her own emotions, memories, and experiences to shape how a character might speak, move, and think. The goal of Method acting is to create three-dimensional characters. Rather than being a stereotype that represents a single concept, such as a villain or a hero, the characters become complex human beings with multiple, even contradictory, feelings and desires.

One of Stanislavski's students, Richard Boleslawsky, brought his teacher's principles to New York City and opened an acting school. The Group Theater was formed in 1931, and since then many famous actors and actresses have studied under the tutelage of equally famous instructors, including Lee Strasberg and Stella Adler.

20s. I said I would give it one more year, but I didn't think I'd make it work. It was out of my control and I'm a control freak,"[30] Bullock says.

The Dangers of City Life

Living in an expensive, fast-paced city like New York was difficult for a struggling actress; not knowing where her next paycheck was coming from was especially unnerving. In addition to being a bartender, Bullock checked coats, and she even managed to get a good job as a waitress at a trendy Italian restaurant on Park Avenue.

One night, after making an impressive $186 in tips, Bullock was walking home when she was held up at gunpoint. She recalls that the man was sweating and that he looked like he had been using drugs. But she wasn't just scared, she was mad. The money in her purse was hard-earned and she wasn't planning to give it to him. Bullock says, "So I was just standing there and I was, 'Well, you're not going to . . . get my money. You're going to have to shoot me in the back.'"[31]

Luckily, Bullock got out of the alley, and New York City, alive. She decided to move to Los Angeles, but not only because of New York's crime rate. After a lot of soul searching, she came to the conclusion that she wanted to be a film actress. So she packed up her old, broken-down Honda and drove three thousand miles across the country in search of her dream.

City of Angels

The City of Angels, as Los Angeles is known, is the center of the entertainment industry. Still chasing her big break, Bullock was determined to get a fresh start in a new town. She was twenty-five years old and a little more seasoned. She knew struggle and rejection but was still determined to be a working actress. Her parents had warned her of the hard times they sometimes endured and told her about the rejection they routinely faced. "Sandy is very aware of the essential fragility of the entire situation of show business," said director Peter Bogdanovich, who later directed her in *The Thing Called Love*. "Her parents are in the business, and she has seen them struggle and never make it the way they would have liked to. She knows the ups and downs."[32]

Bullock was soon on an up. She was cast in several television movies, including *The Preppie Murder* and *Bionic Showdown: The Six Million Dollar Man and the Bionic Woman.* The work led to a steady job on the sitcom *Working Girl,* which was based on the hit film of the same name. Although Bullock knew the series wasn't high art, she was happy to be able to pay her bills after years of struggling. She finally replaced her Honda and started a savings account. At twenty-six, Bullock was a full-time actress and no longer needed to support herself with anything other than acting.

Working Actress

Despite her accomplishments, Bullock admits she hated television work. She claims she found it too confining. What she really wanted was a shot at films. After *Working Girl* was canceled after just one season, Bullock found herself in the position to follow her dream. "I was so glad it failed. I was so unhappy there, I was getting ready to pull a postal worker. It was not funny, but it paid well and I stashed my money away."[33]

After the series was canceled, her first feature film was a B-movie (a film made on a smaller budget with little-known actors, usually in limited release) with director Roger Corman called *Fire on the Amazon.* To Bullock's relief, the film was never released. "I was young and inexperienced, but I was still smart enough to not trust those people, and I insisted on duct tape being placed across my private parts," she later said. "Believe me, you don't see anything of mine in that movie,"[34] she claimed.

After she became famous, Corman said he planned to release the movie, but Bullock wasn't too concerned: "I don't care about how famous I get, nobody is ever going to want to see that movie. It is a horrible piece of garbage."[35]

Love Potions

After a few more disappointing roles in other films, Bullock starred as a nerdy psychobiologist in *Love Potion No. 9.* Although

Sandra Bullock as Tess McGill in the short-lived television sitcom Working Girl. Working Girl*'s cancellation allowed Bullock to pursue film acting.*

the film was a critical and financial flop, it was the best time in Bullock's young life—she was in love. Bullock began dating and soon fell in love with her costar Tate Donovan.

The new couple had a fun time playing two nerds who become popular after drinking a palm reader's secret formula. Crew and castmates, however, were surprised by the union.

A scene from Love Potion No. 9 *with Sandra Bullock and Tate Donovan. The two fell in love while filming the movie.*

They claimed that Tate was what many considered a stereotypical actor, more concerned with his close-up shots. Sandra, on the other hand, was called a sweetheart by the staff. By the end of shooting, however, the two were inseparable. They decided to ignore everyone else but themselves.

For the first time in years, twenty-seven-year-old Bullock was pleased with both her professional and personal life. She was in a good relationship and enjoying acting. The off-screen love story of Sandra and Tate had many reporters asking what kind of love potion he used to win her over. Bullock explained in 1995,

The ability to make me laugh a lot [is important]. Just be very interested in me. Sometimes I'm all over the place. But I'm incredibly loyal, and I don't like it when somebody puts me in a box. Don't say, "Oh she's great, but if I could just calm her down a little bit . . ." I once met an old cowboy. His wife was a free spirit and he was very steady. They'd been married for 40 years. I asked him how it worked. He said, "Well, my dad always told me, You have a wild pony, don't put up a fence. Just leave a light on at home. If she's happy she'll always come home." Same with me: Don't corral me and I'll always come home. Always. Just let me go out and play during the day. When I'm exhausted, I'll come back.[36]

Vanishing Roles

Bullock was far from exhausted with her work, however. She felt as though her career was just getting off the ground. But as soon as it had liftoff, it came crashing back down. During the next year, Sandra had bit parts in two unknown films, *Me and the Mob* and *When the Party's Over*, and then didn't work for months. During this time, she admits that she contemplated giving up acting to work behind-the-scenes, either directing or writing. Luckily, she had Donovan to keep her confident during this dry spell. He encouraged her to keep auditioning.

Love in the Spotlight

Most actors and actresses love their jobs but hate the fact that their personal lives are on display for the world to see. Tate Donovan was the first in a series of Bullock romances that were chronicled by the media, and the scrutiny has made Bullock very wary and frightened of love. As she told *Premiere* magazine in April 2000, "I have a fear of saying the L-word," she admits. "I always feel like the minute I say it, the sky will fall."

Instead of using the "L" word, Bullock uses code. "I've said, 'I adore you,' and that was my way of [saying I love you] . . . because it felt the same and I meant exactly that."

Bullock's persistence paid off when she landed the part of Kiefer Sutherland's girlfriend in 1993's *The Vanishing*. The role was small, her character gets kidnapped in the film's beginning and isn't found until the end, but Bullock felt as though she were warming up for greatness. She was right. The next year—1994 —would forever change the actress's life.

Chapter 3

*Speed*ing Ahead

I<small>N THE MIDST</small> of a career drought, Bullock threw herself into renovating her L.A. apartment. But it wasn't long before she was too busy for work around the house. Bullock soon learned she had won two parts that she'd spent three months auditioning for. One role was as an aspiring country singer in *The Thing Called Love*, River Phoenix's last film before he died. The other was as a waitress whom award-winning actor Robert Duvall has a crush on in *Wrestling Ernest Hemingway*. She called the latter job "one of my favorite experiences in my entire life [something] that you don't expect to happen to you till you're 80." [37]

Just Add Salsa

Bullock and Duvall became good friends on the set of *Wrestling Ernest Hemingway,* despite the thirty-year age difference. Bullock explained that the older actor also helped lead her to one of her life long passions. Between takes, Duvall taught her to merengue, a fast ballroom dance in which the dancers keep one leg stiff. Bullock was intrigued. Soon, she was also being taught the finer points of flamenco, the Spanish-gypsy style of dance that involves stamping and clapping. Both dances fall under the broader category of salsa dancing, which Bullock is now completely hooked on. She claims that it totally relaxes her: "When I'm dancing is when I'm most comfortable with myself, the most free and expressive." [38] She says she has even dedicated a large part of her spacious closet to the outfits she wears when she goes dancing—tight short skirts and high heels. The first thing Bullock now does when she's filming in a new city is find the local salsa joint.

Robert Duvall and Sandra Bullock in Wrestling Ernest Hemingway. *Duvall introduced Bullock to salsa dancing, which quickly became one of her favorite pastimes.*

Fast Friends

Although working with veteran actor Duvall and learning how to salsa was a thrill, Bullock also enjoyed working with other young, up-and-coming stars River Phoenix, Samantha Mathis, and Dermot Mulroney in the film *The Thing Called Love.* Bullock got to write a country song (hers was called "Heaven Knocked on My Door") and even dared sing on set, despite claiming to have a horrible voice. Bullock especially hit it off with actress Samantha Mathis, who was romantically involved with Phoenix.

Shortly after they completed filming in Nashville, Tennessee, Bullock got a telephone call from her mother that Phoenix had died of a drug overdose. She says, "It was one of the scariest experiences I've ever had. My mom called and told me at six in the morning, and for two hours I just let the phone sit in my lap." [39]

After she got over the initial shock, Bullock took Mathis under her wing. The two bonded and became good friends. "I was going through a hard time emotionally and wanted to stay under the covers, but she dragged me out," Mathis remembered. "We'd go shopping. She'd call me up and say, 'I'll be there in 15 minutes.'" [40]

Bullock feared Phoenix's death was a result of the pressures of Hollywood. She said in 1995,

> Young people can get lost (in Hollywood) because they don't have a good foundation, in general. A lot of them come to this because it defines who you are, or to find a place for you. If you're indifferent or unhappy you can just use that in your work. But if you add fame, it's just going to magnify the [problem]. [41]

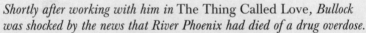

Shortly after working with him in The Thing Called Love, *Bullock was shocked by the news that River Phoenix had died of a drug overdose.*

Going Commercial

After she finished filming *The Thing Called Love*, Bullock decided to make a big, commercial film. Rather than thinking of her decision as selling out, Bullock saw it as a way to expand her horizons and not get pigeon-holed in one genre. She decided she wanted to have fun and do an action film.

Just a week later, the actress was painting the bathroom in her L.A. apartment when she got a call from a producer asking her to costar with Sylvester Stallone in *Demolition Man*. It was the first time Bullock hadn't been asked to audition. She was used to having several callbacks before landing a job and now she was simply being asked to star. An hour after the call she was on the set meeting Sylvester Stallone, star of the *Rocky* series of movies.

Bullock starred opposite Sylvester Stallone in Demolition Man, *her first high-profile movie.*

Soon, Bullock was taking cues from explosions and pieces of moving machinery. "It was a great opportunity," she later said, "even if they chopped off my hair and put me in stretch pants."[42]

Although she admitted to the media that she was nervous for four of the five months of filming, Bullock did bond with her muscular costar. The two were like kids on the set, full of energy and jokes. She says, "We'd knock heads, but at some point, I became like his younger sister. He'd bang on the trailer with his golf clubs in the middle of the night, 'Come and play.' You know, he'd want to swat golf balls in the middle of the night."[43]

Stallone wasn't the only one who wanted to spend time with Bullock. Thanks to her high-profile role, the press was discovering her as well. She found herself granting interviews and appearing in magazines. Reporters were charmed by her manners and humility. "She is the sort of person who thanks you for laughing at her jokes,"[44] claimed one reporter.

Bullock wasn't used to all the attention. After all, it was just a few years before that she'd been doing her own makeup. Now she was being treated like a star. The big-budget film was opening a new world for her. Bullock later remembered one event on *Demolition Man* that made her realize that she'd finally made it in Hollywood. She says,

> [Producer Joel Silver and I] were sitting at the craft service table and I said something about marshmallow fluff. There's two kinds—the glass jar kind, and the plastic jar, which is the best kind. And I was saying that I had not had that stuff for so long and that I had a craving for a fluff sandwich, which is with peanut butter. Pure garbage. Three days later, there's a crate of it in my room. They couldn't get it out in California so they had somebody look for it on the East Coast and flew it out.[45]

The Bus Movie

After *Demolition Man* wrapped, Bullock thought she'd go on to a different type of film. Then her agent told her about a new action movie called *Speed*. Fox Pictures didn't want her for the part, but first-time director Jan De Bont had an instinctual feeling about

Bullock. "She had such an incredible freshness. You really want to be her friend,"[46] he said. When De Bont finally won out and offered Bullock the part, her friends and family warned her not to take it, fearing the part would typecast her as the female sidekick. "Everyone told me not to do it," she remembered. "I mean, it looked like I'd just be 'the girl.' I've learned to do things by instinct."[47]

Bullock's instincts told her that *Speed* was right for her, and she accepted the part. She quickly befriended her costars Keanu Reeves and Dennis Hopper. Filming was intense but enjoyable. Bullock did grow tired, however, of wearing the same bland, baggy tan dress every day during the months of shooting. After just a few days, the shopaholic wanted to burn it.

Speed's story line revolves around an L.A.P.D. SWAT team specialist (Keanu Reeves) who is sent to diffuse a bomb that has been planted on a bus by a revenge-seeking extortionist, played by Dennis Hopper. The catch is that the bus must maintain a speed of fifty miles per hour or the bomb will explode. When the bus driver is shot, Bullock's character takes the wheel.

When *Speed* was released in the summer of 1994, it became a blockbuster, grossing more than $100 million. The film was Bullock's first critical and financial success. "Her chemistry with Keanu Reeves turned out to be more explosive than any bomb Dennis Hopper's terrorist could cook up," wrote one critic at *Entertainment Weekly* magazine. "She upstaged Reeves' buzz cut, Hopper's manic cackling, and Jan De Bont's sleek direction to become the most beloved bus driver since Ralph Kramden [a character on the 1950s TV show *The Honeymooners*]."[48]

Suddenly, Bullock was not in the periphery of the public eye, she was at its center. "Never, in a million years, did I think a bus movie would open every door I ever possibly wanted to have open,"[49] Bullock said in 1995.

A Whole Other Sandra

Right after *Speed* opened in the United States, Bullock went abroad to promote it overseas. "So I wasn't part of the animal I created," she said. "When I came back, it was like there was this whole other me. It was very interesting."[50]

Sandra Bullock and Keanu Reeves, stars of the 1994 blockbuster Speed. *The phenomenal success of* Speed *launched Bullock into stardom.*

Still, Bullock's tight circle of friends and family kept her life feeling pretty normal, much like it had been before. Rather than blow her check on clothes, jewelry, or trips, she used some of her paycheck from the film—a reported $200,000—to buy a Ford Explorer and invested and saved the rest.

She also sunk some cash into the fixer-upper house she and her sister, Gesine, who was in law school, bought in L.A. The whole family would come over and work on projects together. Bullock admitted that she subcontracted out some of the very large and involved projects, but she was determined to do most of the work herself. In fact, she laid each of the tiles in the floor of her Spanish-style kitchen. When she wasn't working in the house, Bullock was out finding just the right furniture to fill it. She couldn't wait to entertain in her new space. As she turned thirty, she'd made it in Hollywood, and she wanted to give back

Awards for "the Girl Next Door"

Even though she was once pigeon-holed as the sweet girl next door, Bullock's work has not gone unhonored. Part of the reason for her success was the string of awards she won after the release of *Speed*. In 1995, she received MTV Movie Awards for Best Female Performance in a movie, Best On-screen Duo (with Keanu Reeves), and Most Desirable Female. She was also awarded the Golden Apple Award for Female Star of the Year and the prestigious NATO/ShoWest Award for Female Star of the Year, which is selected by a board of movie theater owners and operators. Suddenly, Sandra Bullock was a household name. Even with the awards, Bullock can't seem to shake that girl-next-door image. It's a fascination she's never understood. She explained to *Allure* magazine in April 2000,

> I've lived next door to people all my life. I don't know how cute they think I am. When I was little, I didn't really do anything bad—I'd just pull plants out of their yard, pot them, and resell them to them. I made a lot of cash. I'd build skateboard ramps and put on plays and make everyone come, cheesy stuff like that. I was just wild—I didn't mind getting into anything or hooking up with anybody. When we were living in Germany, I was always running around, and my mom said somebody came up to her and asked, "Does anyone know who that gypsy child belongs to?" And my mother was like, "Uh, that's my daughter."

Keanu Reeves and Sandra Bullock won the Best On-screen Duo award for Speed *at the 1995 MTV Movie Awards.*

to all of those who'd helped her get there. In 1995, Bullock explained that she had her friends and family to thank for keeping her grounded and helping her life stay relatively normal:

> My life hasn't really changed in the last year. More people are watching me now, of course, and I can't do things in public that might embarrass me, but that's not my nature anyway. I am reluctant to change. I don't want to change. I guess the question is whether I can maintain my life without sacrificing who I am. I still am the same person I've always been, and that is a person who tends to give people the benefit of the doubt. My friends have tried to change me on that level because I tend to get hurt a lot, but I can't worry about that. If I get hurt, then at least I've tried.[51]

After *Speed*'s success, Bullock found her name on the lists of most Hollywood casting directors. "The good part of fame is that I'm getting to see all the scripts now; not just the action scripts, not just the romantic scripts, but all the scripts,"[52] she said.

Chapter 4

Professional Success/ Personal Unhappiness

I<small>T DIDN'T LOOK</small> as though Sandra Bullock's life could get any better. She was doing what she loved, being well paid for her efforts, and becoming recognized by both her peers and critics. However, just as she was enjoying professional success, the bottom fell out of her nearly four-year relationship with Tate Donovan. "All of a sudden I was watching my whole career unfold while I couldn't keep the other from folding up,"[53] she told reporters after the breakup.

Lost Love

The decision to part was mutual, but that didn't make it any easier. While abroad promoting *Speed*, Bullock often spent her free time on the bathroom floor of various hotel rooms, crying. A romantic at heart, even years after their split, she still considered Donovan her one true love. Though there have been other boyfriends, including another costar, Matthew McConaughey, Bullock saw a real future with Tate.

> He's the greatest human being I ever met. I don't think I'll ever find anybody who fits me like he does. It's very, very, very sad. . . . He really dug deep. He took the most unattractive sides of me and said, "This, I find beautiful." The things that he found to love in me was me being vulnerable, me needing someone.[54]

After her heartbreak, Bullock reassessed what she needed from a relationship. She now admits that blue-collar men (men who do not wear a suit and work in an office) are more appealing to her. She also has her sights set high; she'd rather not settle when it comes to something as important as love. "He has to be very witty, with a sharp sense of humor and be a really good salsa dancer," she explained to a *People* magazine reporter. "And he has to be good with a drill, good around the house. I dated an actor for years. Now it's like—maybe a fisherman." [55]

Bullock with her on- and off-screen love Tate Donovan in Love Potion No. 9. *The couple broke up after a four-year relationship.*

The Two-Week Rule

In 1999, Bullock explained to *E!Online* that she has what she calls a two-week rule when it comes to on-set relationships.

> You're thrown into a situation where you have to create this sort of artificial intimacy with the guys you're costarring with. It's unnatural, because you spend more time with this person than you do with your significant other. I give it two weeks and just observe the person. In the beginning you're going, "Oh, he's so sweet, and he's so attentive, and he's so great." After two weeks, it's like, "Oh, he does this just like everyone else I know." It gives you a new perspective.

The two-week rule has undoubtedly saved Bullock some heartbreak, and it's also helped her make many good friends. By seeing the good and bad in her costars, Bullock is able to accept them for who they are. She has stayed friends with many of the people she's worked with, adding them to her tight circle.

Her insecure side, however, comes out when she thinks about marriage. Bullock has a recurring dream that there's an aisle at the end of a doorway and at the end of the aisle is a tiny groom waiting for her. All she can do is wonder if he is the man she's supposed to marry. She has another version of the dream in which the man she's supposed to marry is in the audience instead of at the altar. Her fears have been ongoing, she explained:

> I have always been petrified of marriage—absolutely afraid. I've felt like once I would get married, someone would want to change me, and I would have no choice but to become this locked-up specimen in a box. I'm worried about losing my freedom of expression. People who meet me go, "Oh, you're really fun and wild." Then as soon as they get to know me, they go, "Well don't do that." And then I don't do it. And I become this separate person from who I was. Then I resent the person who was trying to change me.[56]

Romantic Comedienne

As sad as Bullock was about her breakup with Donovan, the experience helped her in her role as Lucy in the romantic comedy

While You Were Sleeping. She began filming in Chicago in the fall of 1994 and quickly identified with the lonely, single girl in the film. The character hasn't found love and is a hopeless romantic.

The plot of *While You Were Sleeping* revolves around Lucy's loneliness. As a toll taker, she sits in a booth all day and plans a life she isn't living. The only thing that keeps her going is her crush on Peter, a handsome man who gives her his token every day. One day, as Peter waits for the train, two muggers push him onto the tracks and knock him unconscious. Lucy saves him from being hit by an oncoming train, but Peter slips into a coma, and Lucy is mistaken for his fiancée.

Bullock was the last person to read for the part of Lucy, a role that was originally supposed to go to actress Demi Moore. Moore, however, passed on the project, opening the door for Bullock. She still had to audition for the role, but the experience was different from anything she'd experienced before. She explains, "Everybody's sitting there. I've got [producer and Disney chairman] Joe Roth right next to my ear, and I'm talking to this

Bill Pullman and Sandra Bullock in a still from the romantic comedy While You Were Sleeping.

. . . guy in a coma, who's some reader they've brought in. But I loved this film so much, I wasn't nervous."[57]

Producers picked up on her love for the character and story, and the part was hers. The actress was incredibly grateful for the chance to flex her muscles as a romantic leading lady. Appearing on the television show *Live with Regis & Kathie Lee* to promote the film, Bullock displayed her sweetness and sense of humor when she thanked Demi Moore for not taking the role:

Bullock got the opportunity to audition for the part of Lucy in While You Were Sleeping *because Demi Moore (pictured) passed on the role.*

"I just want to thank her, thank her for being busy and letting me have this. I'm so grateful, I gave her half my check. She bought a new dress."[58]

A Friend in Need

Bullock's paycheck for *While You Were Sleeping* may have been many times less than what Moore might have pulled in at the time, but it was still substantial enough for her to be generous. On the film's set, she threw a Halloween party at a Chicago club. The theme, appropriately enough for *While You Were Sleeping*, was a pajama party. She hired a salsa band and footed the bill for the cast and crew.

Even though Bullock felt as though she was getting some good acting parts, she wanted to take control of her career in another way: by starting her own production company. In 1994, she formed Fortis (meaning strength and perseverance in Latin) Films. She immediately hired her best friend from college to help run it. "He's reading all my scripts. He's helping assist me in my daily life,"[59] she explained.

Bullock helped another friend from New York sell his screenplay. She brought the script, *Kate and Leopold*, to her agent, Tom Chestaro, and asked him to represent her friend. The script not only sold to Miramax and came out in 1997, but featured Bullock as a scientist who deals with an eighteenth-century English nobleman transported to modern-day Manhattan.

Praise for Sandra

Bullock was wielding more power than she had ever anticipated in Hollywood. After the spring 1995 release of *While You Were Sleeping*, some critics called her the next Julia Roberts. She appeared alongside Uma Thurman, Nicole Kidman, and Sarah Jessica Parker on the cover of *Vanity Fair*'s annual up-and-comers issue. She was also one of *Entertainment Weekly* magazine's Entertainers of the Year for 1995, and one of *People*'s Top 10 Players Under 35 in 1996.

Each deemed her one to watch in the future, and Bullock was amazed at her success. Not everyone was surprised, however.

People who had worked with Bullock knew she was going places. "She has this bravado,"[60] said Micole Mercurio, who worked with her on both *While You Were Sleeping* and *Wrestling Ernest Hemingway.* That bravado, coupled with inherent talent, made it possible for her to take the risks she needed to move her career forward.

On the heels of Bullock's success came another leading role in 1995's *The Net.* Although it was considered an action film, *The Net* was really a thriller. Its plot, about a woman whose identity is stolen, scared Bullock because the situation seemed possible. She explained,

> This isn't just another thriller. This is intended as a cautionary tale. The whole Big Brother theory is being played out right now, and people deserve to know that. It's happening to us already, but I'm not sure how to stop it. Every time you use your credit card, you're adding one more bit of information about your habits and lifestyle into the computer. I guess the answer . . . is to pay cash and don't own anything, but is that really a solution? Is that any way to live?[61]

Director Irwin Winkler was impressed with Bullock's interpretation of the role and with her personality once the cameras stopped rolling. She was typically down-to-earth and friendly. "Sandra doesn't have a star attitude. People see a lot of themselves in her,"[62] he said.

Winkler wasn't the only one she charmed on the set. The crew loved her too. She invited them along with her to salsa clubs in L.A. Rather than asking them to fetch her coffee, she spent many mornings running out for cappuccinos for everyone. She even shared her private and beloved junk-food stash. The crew, in turn, made a tribute to Bullock, creating a montage of clips of the star set to the tune of the song "I've Grown Accustomed to Her Face." When they showed it at the film's wrap party, Bullock was in tears. She had grown so close to the crew, she even asked technician Don Padilla (who was rumored to be her boyfriend) to escort her to *The Net*'s premiere.

Sandra Bullock plays a computer expert whose identity is stolen in the 1995 thriller The Net.

With the success of the film, Sandra's asking price rose to $6 million. Despite saying she would take time off after the movie, Bullock signed on to do three more films: the adaptation of John Grisham's novel *A Time to Kill*, the romantic comedy *Two If by*

Sandra Bullock at the premiere of The Net. *Bullock attended the premiere with Don Padilla, a technician from* The Net*'s crew.*

Sea, and *Kate and Leopold.* Bullock was now one of the most prolific actresses in Hollywood, and she seemed to have a good grasp on her thriving career. She said,

> I want everything to be completely different than the last thing I did. I never want to give anyone the chance

to stereotype me. If anyone's going to do any stereotyping around here, it's going to be me. . . . It's still early enough in my career that I just want to surprise people. It's easy for me to do comedy and it's become a safety net, and that's why I want to do new things. Not only to surprise the audience, but to see whether I can do it.[63]

By then, Bullock had millions of fans. She was accustomed to stopping every day to sign autographs and pose for pictures. Her life had become everything she dreamed of and more. After endless auditions and more rejections than she cared to remember, Bullock had made it.

Letting Go

However, the time had come for some changes in her life. Bullock no longer saw eye to eye with her manager, Tom Chestaro, and after twelve years together, she let him go. She was upset at having to take the action and doesn't discuss the details of the split.

Soon after Chestaro was fired, Bullock hired her father to manage her. The media suggested that John Bullock was controlling and that he might have been behind the termination of Chestaro. John shrugged off the rumors, however, and set to work helping his daughter and Fortis Films. "I have no personal agenda, except her happiness,"[64] he told reporters.

A Road Trip

To get a new perspective, Bullock sometimes calls on her close friends for a much-needed break. In the summer of 1995, she and her pals rented an RV van, piled in the music and food, and headed out on the open road. Although she'd traveled all over Europe, until this time, Bullock had seen very little of the United States. She and six friends drove across country, stopping at all of her most desired destinations. They went to Graceland (the home of Elvis Presley) in Memphis, Tennessee, and gambled a bit in Las Vegas, Nevada. It was on this trip that Bullock discovered her present hometown of Austin, Texas. Along the way, they didn't stay at the luxury hotels to which stars can grow accustomed. In fact, the cost-conscious Motel 6 was their favorite place to stay the night.

Bullock loved working with her father. He helped her organize her finances and plan what to do with her earnings. She immediately called her dad for reassurance and guidance.

With more than ten films under her belt, thirty-two-year-old Sandra Bullock was feeling both fortunate and accomplished. She was also looking for a new challenge.

Chapter 5

New Roles

SOON AFTER HER change in management, Bullock took on some different kinds of roles. She played a gum-chewing girlfriend of an art thief in *Two If by Sea* and a politically minded law student in *A Time to Kill*. She also began working on her own short independent films.

On the acting front, Bullock next decided to play an early-twentieth-century nurse who falls for a young Ernest Hemingway in the film *In Love and War*. She chose the film because the character was a complete departure from her own personality. "Everything I know about myself had to leave. That's why I did it," [65] she said.

A New Kind of Performance

For the part of Hemingway's love, Agnes von Kurowsky, Bullock did lots of preparation. She gained weight for the part—something she didn't find too challenging given her penchant for junk food. In between meals, Bullock also conducted more research than she ever had before. She did a lot of reading, took diction lessons, and was given instruction in body movement. She even watched gruesome operations and memorized the 1918 Red Cross's nurses' handbook in order to learn how medicine was practiced in the early twentieth century. She called the film the most mentally challenging one she'd ever done, saying

> It was a definite transformation of everything that I knew as comfortable, that we sort of removed and started from scratch. And you have someone like [director] Richard [Attenborough] to guide you. A lot of directors say "trust

me" and then they let you fall on your face. In this case, you knew when he said "trust me," you could go back and look at the body of work he had pulled out of others, and the abandonment was a lot easier. It was a feat, but a welcome one.[66]

Working with the great British director Sir Richard Attenborough was both awe-inspiring and challenging for the actress. "Sir Richard promised that 'Sandra Bullock' would not be in the movie, and that's what I wanted," Bullock told *People* magazine after filming was complete. "My performance was based on listening rather than constantly running off at the mouth. Whenever I let some of that contemporary woman show, he'd stand by the camera and trace a big B [for Bullock] in the air. I would know that 'she' was in the building and needed to be kicked out."[67]

The role of an early-twentieth-century nurse in In Love and War *was a challenge for Bullock.*

Sir Richard Attenborough directed Bullock in In Love and War *and deemed her performance "exquisite."*

In order to lose herself in the character, Bullock relied on the costumes. She told the media that the petticoats, corsets, stockings, and boots made her feel different, more like Agnes. The wardrobe affected her movement, the way she sat and stood, making her more refined and conscious of her body.

Shooting in Italy, where the film takes place, also set her in the right frame of mind for the part. She no longer felt like a modern woman but more of an early-twentieth-century female. She explained, "The streets and the atmosphere: you have a sense of timelessness and you don't have contemporary apparatuses. We didn't even want to watch TV; anything that was modern you just didn't want." [68]

All the work Bullock did in preparing and listening paid off. She delivered a performance that pleased the film's producers and director. "I felt she was capable of more refined acting than anything she has done before this," Attenborough explained. "And that's what happened. She was exquisite." [69]

Although overwhelming at times, the part was also incredibly satisfying. Bullock was slowly overcoming any fears and insecurities she had in terms of taking on new and different characters.

A Few Bombs

Despite Attenborough's praise, *In Love and War* wasn't very well received at the box office. *Two If by Sea* was also panned by critics. Her next flick, *Speed 2: Cruise Control,* bombed as well, although traveling to the beautiful island of St. Martin for months of filming was a plus. Bullock rented a house on the water and invited friends to visit.

Even though her movies weren't being praised, Bullock was credited with good performances. "It's easy to understand why Bullock is one of the day's hottest stars. She is flat out adorable," wrote a critic at *People Weekly,* about *Two If by Sea.* "One suspects [her costar Denis] Leary was going after a bitter social comedy about class structure. . . . Instead, this is merely a conventional romantic comedy with Bullock the saving grace—except not enough of one to save it." [70]

To Bullock, her failures were even successes. She wasn't upset by the few "bombs," or bad pictures. Instead, they make her appreciate the good films she's made even more. She has learned

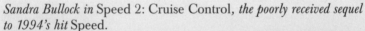

Sandra Bullock in Speed 2: Cruise Control, *the poorly received sequel to 1994's hit* Speed.

from her mistakes and insists that they have only improved her work. She says,

> I look back on certain choices that I made, and wonder if I did it out of the working actor's desperation to just take anything that comes along. I allowed myself, several times, to be mediocre. I'm very well aware of that, and [those films] are good reminders to look back and say, "Don't do that." And it's halfway out of trying to be pleasing to everybody. You find mediocrity that way. I'm not going to allow myself to be mediocre or anything that I'm involved with to be mediocre.[71]

Different Kinds of Films

By 1997, Bullock was ready for a change. She decided to take some time off from big-budget flicks, instead opting to direct and produce a short film she also wrote called *Making Sandwiches*. She played Melba to Matthew McConaughey's Bud. Together, they portray a married couple who run a small-town coffee shop. Their relationship is threatened, however, when a new shop opens. Bullock explains,

> It's a very American metaphor of two slices of bread, and whatever you put in between is up to you and how ritualistic we become in our relationships. And that can be a good thing, but if you don't allow for expansion between those two slices of bread, there is going to be a rift when someone grows. It's just about the simplicity of life and what happens if you allow the slices to get further and further or closer and closer together depending upon what your appetite is.[72]

Filming *Making Sandwiches* was a challenge for Bullock, but she also considers it one of her happiest times. Instead of just being in front of the camera, she was also behind it, making decisions and footing the bill for the shoot. *Forbes* magazine ranked her fortieth on its annual list of top-paid entertainers for 1996, and she was grateful that her acting was funding her latest love.

She found herself even more interested in what was going on behind the camera than in front of it. She explains,

> I don't need more money. I don't need more attention on myself. Producing is very rewarding. It makes me feel like a proud parent. You'll be there at two in the morning, behind the monitor with greasy hair and then the actors will do something that just inspires you.[73]

Making Sandwiches wasn't the first time Bullock had tried her hand at making a movie. Two years earlier, she had recruited a group of friends to make *The Mailman*, a film about a postal worker who goes crazy. She got the chance to screen both films at the Sundance Film Festival, one of the most prestigious annual gatherings for actors and filmmakers.

In the next movie she made, audiences couldn't even see her. *The Prince of Egypt* is an animated version of the story of Moses and was directed and produced by Steven Spielberg, who made *Schindler's List* and *Saving Private Ryan*. Most actresses would have jumped at the chance to work with Spielberg, but Bullock needed some coaxing to lend her voice to the character Miriam. Ultimately, she was convinced. "Steven Spielberg called and asked me to do it," she said. "Then I talked to [Spielberg's partner] Jeffrey Katzenberg. Those guys can get you to do anything."[74]

Working on an animated film was quite different from live action, as Bullock soon found out. "You don't have the atmosphere of being on a movie set," she explains. "You're in a little recording booth with no crutches [other actors or props]. It's like being there naked with your voice."[75]

Deep in the Heart of Texas

Bullock felt fortunate to have a job she loved and friends she cared about, but after almost four years in the limelight, the pressure of always being in the spotlight was starting to take its toll. She admits that she never feels comfortable dressed up at a party or premiere. She'd rather be in jeans, drinking a beer at a barbecue in her own backyard. The problem, though, was that Bullock's backyard was L.A., too close to the pressures she was trying to escape. She decided to buy another home that she could escape to when she needed a break.

Years earlier, on a cross-country road trip with friends, Bullock had fallen in love with Austin, Texas. It was just the right mix of down-home country flavor, wide open spaces, and a fairly cosmopolitan major city. "Austin has its own rhythm going. You never know when you're going to fall in love; you don't expect it. And I fell in love with Austin,"[76] she claimed.

Although the media began to wonder if her choice in a new hometown had anything to do with her boyfriend Matthew McConaughey being from Austin, she insisted it did not. Bullock bought some land and set to work building her dream house. The move to the country turned out to be the right one for Bullock. It rejuvenated her and allowed her to step back from her crazy life. She says,

A view of the city skyline and Colorado River in Austin, Texas. The city appealed to Bullock, who bought land in the area and built a house.

Building Her Dream House

When Sandra Bullock decided to build a house in Austin, she described her dream home as a Texas meets French Provincial farmhouse. Her desire was to have something functional as well as aesthetically pleasing. Most of all, she wanted a place to relax and kick-back. Bullock met with architects and interior designers to create the right space and the right look.

She described her plans for the house to *InStyle* magazine in May 1998. She even invited them back after its completion to take pictures. "I want a huge living room that is basically a dance floor . . . a big farmhouse kitchen with wide-plank floors and a fireplace and a table that will accommodate 20." Bullock also envisioned a big stone barbecue pit off the back patio and a boat for the lake bordering her backyard. "The house itself, the structure, should be art . . . comfortable and conducive to living. . . . I want my house to be ones of those places you can walk in and get dirt on the couch, where the dogs can run around."

Later that year, Bullock and her three dogs were doing just that. The house turned out just the way she had planned. She set to work filling it with a collection of antiques as well as thrift-store finds, including an old bear-claw bathtub she found at a junkyard in Reno, Nevada. She wanted to make the mix of furniture funky and eclectic, even adding to one room a hula-girl lamp that gyrates when the light comes on. Bullock was so happy with her house and Austin that she decided it would be the place she retires when she's old and gray.

I'm a bit odd. I'm a basic person. I like basic food, simple tastes. I like things I understand, things (and people) I can identify with and not have to question their motives. My friends and parents are brutally honest and you always know where you stand. . . . I'm one of those people who used to be really worried about what everybody thought and once I started getting my feelings hurt a lot I said, "You know what? I've got to get over it," so I just isolated myself from it.[77]

Not only did Bullock gain a renewed perspective on life, she also developed one for her career. She decided it was time to get back in the game of making movies.

Hollywood Moves East

As both producer and star of her next film, *Hope Floats*, Bullock chose to film in Austin. *Hope Floats* focuses on Birdee Pruitt (played by Bullock), a former high school cheerleader and homecoming queen who moves back to her hometown in Texas with her young daughter. The script was one Bullock liked from the start. Birdee was a woman struggling to be brave and take chances. She had been hurt by a man, but her family and friends were helping her get back on her own two feet.

A scene from Hope Floats *shows Sandra Bullock with Mae Whitman, who played her daughter. Bullock produced as well as starred in the 1998 film.*

Bullock had to fight to get the picture made. *Hope Floats* was filmed as a result of an earlier deal she made with 20th Century Fox. Bullock agreed to make *Speed 2* only if she could choose her next project and get financial backing from the studio. "It's not that I have clout," she explained, "but that I've been given a lot of liberties right now. If I don't make the best and most of these liberties, I shouldn't have them." [78]

As Bullock turned thirty-four, in the summer of 1998, she finally began to glimpse personal and professional satisfaction. She says,

> As long as I have complete peace of mind, I don't care what people do to me or say about me. Whatever this steamroller called fame turns out to be, I am happy knowing that I am doing nothing to put gas in that steamroller. I'm just moving along doing the most honest work I can do and not worrying about the other things, I never think about salary, and I never think about the trappings of stardom. [79]

Before she even finished *Hope Floats*, Bullock was working on her next projects, the films *Practical Magic* and *Forces of Nature*. She'd been so busy working that she was just starting to realize how popular she had become with entertainment and fashion magazines. She had been on countless covers and chronicled in many fashion spreads. Despite her notions that she was less than fashionable, Sandra Bullock was becoming an icon of style.

Chapter 6

Sandra Style

WHETHER SHE LIKED it or not, fame changed Bullock's life. People were looking at her, scrutinizing what she did, what she wore, and how she styled her hair. In 1997, fans cheered when she picked up the People's Choice Award for Favorite Motion Picture Actress and the Blockbuster Entertainment Award for Favorite Actress in a Suspense Film for *A Time to Kill.* Many, though, were more concerned with what the actress was wearing than with whether or not she won an award.

Three Sides of Sandra

Bullock wasn't used to having her outfits judged and imitated, but that was just what was happening. In 1995, she did a fashion shoot for *Elle* magazine, and fans fell in love with Bullock's down-to-earth attitude toward clothes. She wasn't high style, preferring broken-in Wranglers to a pair of high-fashion Calvin Klein jeans.

The *Elle* fashion spread was also a learning experience for Bullock. During the shoot, she decided she wouldn't be trading in her actress status for model anytime soon. She says, "I dread photo shoots so much—they're nothing like making a film. In front of a movie camera you never have to struggle to emote, but with a still camera you do, and you feel so false some-times." [80]

Bullock claims to have three completely different sides when it comes to dressing: the tailored, classic Audrey Hepburn look (for example, a tailored sheath dress with pumps and pearls); a hippie, earthy style (mixing various bold prints in flowing fabrics topped off with sandals); and dressing like a kid in overalls and

Sandra Bullock's clothing tastes fit her relaxed, fun-loving lifestyle.

a t-shirt. Although her mother's sense of style may have embarrassed her when she was younger, she now enjoys raiding her mother's closet to duplicate her eclectic look.

Bullock prefers comfort and being herself over becoming a slave to fashion. "I'm a comfort person. I like looking a little bit disheveled. I'm a little wild, and for me, clothes need to be able to move, to shed layers. Anything too perfect or controlled is old-fashioned,"[81] she said.

Who's That Guy?

In addition to the scrutiny over what she wears to a party or premiere, there's also the matter of who she brings. Bullock knows that if reporters catch her with anyone, they will immediately assume the two are a couple, even if they are just friends. "It's like

Sandra Bullock and Matthew McConaughey arrive at the premiere of In Love and War *in Los Angeles.*

I meet some guy and say, 'I've only known you for two days, but do you want to go to a premiere so the tabloids can hound you for a month? Yes, let me shatter your life with one walk down that carpet.'"[82]

The tabloids hounded Bullock for months after she was spotted with actor Matthew McConaughey. Neither star ever appeared in public with anyone else of the opposite sex, only fueling rumors that they were an item. After repeatedly denying that they were a couple, Bullock eventually gave up trying to explain their relationship. She did not, however, deny her admiration for him. "He's an exceptional human being, and he is so talented and raw; he doesn't make any excuses. He's become a powerful force in my life. We have fabulous chemistry together,"[83] she said.

Later, Bullock admitted she had had a relationship with McConaughey, but hadn't wanted to discuss it openly as she had done with her relationship with Tate Donovan. "Matthew was just coming into his own. I didn't want him to have that stigma of being my boyfriend," she claims. "I never said, 'We're just friends.' I said, 'We're friends.' And we were friends! I never put a just in there, because I didn't want to, like, really be lying."[84] She simply wanted to keep her private life private.

Beauty: Inside and Out

Much to her surprise, in 1996 and 1999, Bullock was named to *People* magazine's annual list of the 50 Most Beautiful People. She credited any beauty that came through, however, to her team. "That's the great thing about being an actress," she says. "I have this construction crew that can come in, put up some cones around me and work on the disaster area."[85]

Although many people see her as beautiful, Bullock disagrees. She says that her thick brown hair is often a mess, and her nearsightedness has led to a collection of dozens and dozens of pairs of eyeglasses. But the 5'8" actress claims her laugh is what ruins her flawless facade. "It's obnoxious, kind of like a hyena. People complain about it all the time."[86]

Still, laughter breeds a good attitude, and Bullock's good attitude draws other people to her. "She's so very beautiful," said

Sandra on Fashion and Fashion Mistakes

Although she has a good sense of personal style, Bullock does look to others for advice. She told *Allure* magazine in April 2000,

> You see someone like Gwyneth [Paltrow] or whoever looking great and you say, "That's great, I would look good in that, too." They're great marketing tools because I'll buy whatever they have on. But one day I decided, "I like what I like to wear and I know what I look good in. It's not a lot of things, but I know those few things and I'll stick with them." It's like I grew into my own skin and I know the clothes that make me feel comfortable and sexy.

Bullock hasn't always had such an independent outlook on fashion, and she's made more than her share of mistakes. Unlike most people, however, her mistakes often make the front page. She revealed to *Allure*,

> There's one dress in particular from what my friends and I call the Pink Walrus Period. I gained about 15 pounds for my part in *In Love and War* [1997], and I decided to wear a pink satin Calvin Klein dress for the premiere. But I'd been measured for the dress months before, so I had to pour myself into it. I was busting out at the seams—I was a fat, shiny, pink walrus.

her *Hope Floats* costar Harry Connick Jr. "She's got this friendly, laid-back feel, which is very sexy. And she's got such beautiful skin. It's like porcelain. You can't see the pores."[87]

Sandra's Favorite Things

Beauty and laughter are two of her strongest attributes. This does not mean she is without weakness, and Bullock readily admits her vices: blackjack, books, and baths.

She got hooked on blackjack during a trip to Las Vegas. After learning the rules and the object of the game, Bullock began to play. She explains,

> When I was in Reno it became my game of choice. It was the only thing that gave me some sense of control. I had read a little book on how to play blackjack—not

that I remembered anything. I figured that if I could maintain my $35, which I did for an hour—win-lose, win-lose—I was doing well. My one rule was not to look at the ball [where security cameras were rolling] overhead and wave. In fact, they ask you not to. The [security] guy who's watching doesn't want you to say hi. I always take a hit on 17. Always. You're not supposed to, but it's that fine line. I just figure the [gambling] gods like me enough to give me whatever I need. It usually never happens.[88]

After a rough day of shooting a film or losing at the black-jack table, Bullock likes to pamper herself with a bath. She insists on taking two baths a day and doesn't see the shower as a replacement. "If I can only take a shower, it ruins my day," she admitted. "I have so many products around me in the tub—candles and soaps. And I have a conditioner that makes me smell like Pez."[89]

Books are also a favorite source of relaxation for the star. She loves the children's writer Dr. Seuss and collects first editions of his work. In general, Bullock isn't picky about what she reads. And once she picks something up, she never puts it down. She told *Entertainment Weekly* in 1995,

When I start a book, I become obsessed with it—I'm up at 5 a.m. finishing it. There are four books I've started that are unfinished, and I have to go back home because I feel like I have all these relationships that are unresolved; there are all of these books that are unfinished. I want to close the relationship and put it back on the shelf. Sometimes everything in my life is about the book I'm reading.[90]

In the Public Eye

Although she sometimes just wants to curl up at home with a good book, Bullock realizes that her public persona is part of fame. She needs to stay in the spotlight to get good roles and vice versa. Over time, she's gotten more comfortable with fame

Famous children's writer Dr. Seuss is one of Bullock's favorite authors.

but would prefer to have a private life. But that's a hard task to accomplish when the media is constantly misquoting her. She claims,

> I swear to God, nothing that has been printed about me in the last few years has been true. But, there's always, like, a quote or a semi-quote that you know you've said to somebody at sometime—and that's what freaks you out. There's a smidgen of truth in there somewhere. . . . I've never been public about my relationships. I'd say 85 percent of what's out there is not even true. It's just someone with a typewriter needing a story. Katharine Hepburn said a great thing: "I don't care what people write about me as long as it's not true."[91]

Internet Adoration

With the evolution of the Internet, there have been many websites created dedicated to Bullock, and she has personally visited many of the sites while surfing the Web. She does admit, however, that some sites have manufactured pictures of her, posting her face on another woman's nude body. Bullock jokes, however, that as long as the pictures are complimentary—and everyone realizes they are not actually her—she doesn't mind them too much. Her family and friends tease her about them. And her father even printed out one picture as a joke. Bullock's take on the sites is that, with so much going right in her life, it's hard to get upset by some fans' strange methods of adoration.

Bullock has even given her friends permission to fool the media, if they so choose. One of her friends has a picture of her where she looks pregnant. If he ever needs money, Bullock says he just needs to tell her when it's appearing and in what magazine.

Although she's clearly a star, Bullock prides herself in the fact that she still likes the same things she did before she hit it big. Shopping, reading, and playing blackjack filled her free time even before she became a household name. Thanks to her bigger paycheck, however, Bullock can spend more money when she goes shopping and doesn't have to worry if she loses at blackjack.

Chapter 7

Practically Magic

W HEN *SPEED* WAS released in 1994, it changed Bullock's life. For the actress, the most exciting change was the availability of new and interesting scripts. She had enough influence to decide which roles were right for her.

Fans, also, were interested in Bullock's choices. Most of her movies attracted a loyal fan base, and in 1999 they awarded her the People's Choice Award for Favorite Motion Picture Actress. With fans watching her every move, as well as her every movie, Bullock decided to make her career something magical.

Casting a Spell

Bullock and her team at Fortis Films reviewed hundreds of scripts, looking for her next feature. They found it in *Practical Magic*. Based on Alice Hoffman's book of the same name, *Practical Magic* is the story of two sisters who happen to be witches. Bullock both starred in and produced this film, whose cast included Aidan Quinn, Stockard Channing, and Nicole Kidman.

Filming the picture was fun for Bullock, who was proud of the fact that the film would boast two leading ladies on its promotional poster. It's very rare for two women to carry a picture in Hollywood. Bullock and Kidman, however, were rare exceptions of female power and box office draw. They were also a dynamic duo on the set, constantly playing pranks and bonding just like real-life sisters.

In one scene, the two awaken at midnight to the sound of blenders. They go downstairs to indulge in some margaritas with their aunts and end up dancing around the kitchen to the 1970s tune "Coconut." Traditionally, people do not actually

Bullock accepts her award for Favorite Motion Picture Actress at the 1999 People's Choice Awards.

drink alcohol on camera. They may have apple juice instead of beer or grape juice for wine. Bullock and Kidman, however, thought it would be more fun to have real margaritas, so they spiked the mixture. By the time the scenes were complete, all four actresses were tipsy—but the scene was perfect.

Unfortunately, all the fun on the set didn't translate into good reviews for the picture. Critics panned the film, and the movie didn't do well at the box office. "The spoon in Sandra

Bullock's coffee goes round and round all by itself. That one, lonely little gag may just be the only supernatural gambit of any wit or imagination in *Practical Magic,* a witch comedy so slapdash, plodding, and muddled it seems to have had a hex put on it,"[92] wrote a reviewer for *Entertainment Weekly* magazine.

Despite the bad reviews, Bullock didn't regret making *Practical Magic,* because she was developing a good female fan base and being a good role model for young girls. "Having girls as fans is the greatest compliment in the world,"[93] she said.

A Force to Be Reckoned With

Bullock was well aware of her reputation as America's sweetheart, but in her next role she challenged that perception. In *Forces of Nature,* she plays a free spirit who befriends a young groom-to-be on his way to his wedding in Savannah, Georgia. When their plane is forced to make an emergency landing, the two are stuck together through a series of mishaps.

Before she committed to the film, Bullock met with her costar Ben Affleck to make sure they would enjoy working together. "It's important to meet your male lead before you do a film like this," she explained. "You have to be confident that

Nicole Kidman and Sandra Bullock star as sibling witches in Practical Magic. *Despite bad reviews, Bullock was proud of the film.*

you're going to be able to find something to adore about that person."[94]

Bullock found lots to adore about Affleck, and the admiration was mutual. "She's what you want from a leading lady," Affleck said. "She's willing to make fun of herself and you and the situation."[95]

Bullock found the role and making fun of herself liberating. She liked flexing her acting muscles and not being concerned about everyone's perception of her character. She told *Harper's Bazaar* in 1999,

> I loved being someone who wasn't sweet, someone who didn't take care of everyone. My character is . . . a little wild—that was really liberating. For once I didn't have a director telling me, "Well, you really can't do that because we want you to be likable."[96]

Sandra Bullock and Ben Affleck in Forces of Nature. *The wild side of Bullock's character provided a welcomed break from her usual roles.*

She also found that playing an empowered woman on film gave her power in her own life. During the filming of *Forces of Nature*, Bullock shed her wholesome image on- and off-screen. She says, "I sort of became an insane, wild person, a little like her," she explained. "I have that side of myself, and off-camera, I found myself indulging in the luxury of going, 'I can do whatever I want and get into whatever trouble I want.' I found myself doing things like jumping on the back of a motorcycle or staying in a bar way too late. The movie just sort of opened up that side of me. In the process, I guess, I learned that I just don't have enough fun. I need to have a little more."[97]

Apparently, fans are happy to see Bullock in whatever role she chooses. In the summer of 1999, her performance in *Forces of Nature* won her the Teen Choice Award for Best Hissy Fit. Friend Matthew McConaughey presented her with the prize—a surfboard.

She didn't hit the waves right away, however. Instead, Bullock decided she needed a little break. She was feeling the first signs of burnout and wanted to have a normal life for a little while. She says,

> I realized there are so many things I haven't done. I've always wanted to study another language and train for a marathon. I've been working so hard to improve myself in my work and career that I sort of forgot the other things in life that would improve me, I just felt this huge void because I felt most comfortable on a film set. I was missing out on real life.[98]

Bullock ran every day and studied up on foreign languages (other than German). She also spent time with her dogs and her family and friends. After a few months, she was ready for action again.

Fortis at the Forefront

When she returned from her self-imposed break, Bullock had projects lined up and waiting for her attention. The first, *Gun Shy*, was the story of a drug enforcement officer and a mob boss.

Bullock arrives at the 1999 Teen Choice Awards, where she won the Best Hissy Fit award for Forces of Nature.

Bullock took a supporting role in the film but was very involved in its production. *Gun Shy,* according to Bullock, is a chick flick for guys. Although reviews for the film weren't stellar, they were mildly enthusiastic. "*Gun Shy* is worth at least a shot at a matinee,"[99] wrote a critic for the website *Mr. Showbiz.*

However, there was good news even before the film was released. Bullock reportedly negotiated two films with Warner Brothers for Fortis to produce: *Miss Congeniality,* a slapstick comedy along the lines of *Dumb and Dumber* that revolves around a beauty pageant, and *The List,* a romantic comedy about a woman who wants to marry her longtime boyfriend. The latter script was the second wedding-related one Bullock had purchased. She also bought the rights to and plans to star in and produce *Exactly 3:30,* a story about a habitually late woman planning her wedding. She chose each of the scripts because she liked the story and the writing.

In September 1999, before the ink was even dry on the contracts for *Miss Congeniality, The List,* and *Exactly 3:30,* Bullock signed another production deal with Warner Brothers to produce two animated and two live-action projects. She was especially excited about the new challenges that would present themselves in making the animated children's films. *Nicholas Cricket* is a film adaptation of the William Joyce book, in which the lead cricket overcomes a broken heart and helps his ex-girlfriend battle a gang of evil wasps. The other animated movie, *Jingle,* is a Christmas story about the world's most sarcastic elf who has just a few months to change the ways of the world's naughtiest little girl.

One of the two live-action films, *Babe Behind Bars,* was also set to have Bullock star. Both *Babe Behind Bars* and the other, *Alison's Starting to Happen,* are about a subject near to Bullock's heart—careful driving. In *Babe Behind Bars,* the main character, a ruthless Hollywood executive, is sentenced to life in prison after running down an elderly person, leaving the victim in a coma. The story focuses on her life without her power or possessions. *Alison's Starting to Happen* tells the story of a woman who dies in a car crash and then must find meaning in her life in order to get into heaven. Bullock believes that the way people drive says something about who they are. She told a reporter,

> My mother gave me one piece of advice: "Be careful how someone drives you because that's how they'll drive with you in their friendship or relationship." And she'd been absolutely right! If somebody's reckless with you and they're behind the wheel they obviously don't think enough of you to be careful in the car. People curse my mom for this, but that's about the best secret of life anybody's ever given me.[100]

In the April 2000 release of *28 Days*, Bullock's character is also a bad driver. After getting caught driving under the influence at her sister's wedding, her character, a newspaper columnist, is forced into a rehabilitation program, where she meets a handsome baseball player who helps her change her cynical attitude about life.

After she read the script, Bullock knew she wanted to play the part, but she was concerned that the producers were asking her to star in it for the wrong reason. "I've been in enough films where the studio wanted that extra little cuteness to make it sellable," she says. "It destroyed what the film was, and the film bombed."[101] To be sure about the motives, she kept asking the film's director if she were really right for the part.

Betty Thomas, the director of *28 Days*, was more than certain that only Sandra Bullock could pull it off. "I don't think it's that easy to make a comedy-drama out of this subject. So you need the girl next door, okay?" she says. "It's Sandy. She seems like the most normal woman in the world. Which means that everybody is susceptible to this. . . . You knock them for a loop."[102]

Sandy's Success

Over the years, Bullock has gone from a girl in the back of the opera to a star carrying multi-million-dollar films. Along the

Playing Against Type in *28 Days*

To research the role of her alcoholic character in *28 Days*, Bullock and director Betty Thomas conducted research at an actual rehabilitation center. As she had done with *In Love and War*, Bullock delved deep to get at the heart of her character. In an interview with *Premiere* magazine in April 2000, Bullock said,

Understandably, it was really hard for any [rehab center] to let an actress go in to do a little research. . . . But we found a great place where a counselor said it was OK to come into the group, and I entered as though I was one of them. A lot of people in the group were really angry—one woman left. The only way I figured I could do this honestly was to go in as though I was there for a reason. Everything there is based on confidentiality . . . so I figured, "What have I got to lose?" When I left the group, I kind of didn't want to go. I'd started this, I'd opened up a lot of things for me, and I kind of wanted to finish.

Sandra Bullock's healthy attitude allows her to keep mistakes as well as successes in perspective.

way, she's discovered herself through the characters she plays. Although she may have some of the girl next door in her, she's also a free spirit, a caregiver, and someone with a few magical tricks up her sleeve. She enjoys playing different roles—in both her personal and professional life. But she does understand the difference between acting and life:

> My failure, my disappointments, have never come from work. If a film doesn't do well . . . you have another time to try to do better. There's nothing you can do about it after the fact. But how do I bounce back from things that happen in life? I'm not sure. It's not a mistake if you learn from a disappointment and try not to repeat it. That's sort of the mantra I try to use. It's okay to [mess] up even on a daily basis as long as you don't keep repeating the same [mistakes]. I suppose you bounce back by just figuring it's for a reason and it happened to take you to a better place.[103]

Sandra Bullock's mistakes have brought her to a better place. She has friends and family who help her run a successful company. She owns three homes and can financially provide for herself and her loved ones. She feels passionate about her work and ambitions. She doesn't take herself or her fame too seriously. Perhaps most important, she realizes how lucky she is to have everything she does. In 1995, as her career was just getting off the ground, she told a reporter, "Life is good, big time." [104]

Notes

Introduction: "The Girl Next Door"

1. Quoted in Gregory Cerio, "Speeding Bullock," *People Weekly*, August 14, 1995, p. 64.
2. Quoted in Rebecca Ascher-Walsh, "Sandra Bullock," *Entertainment Weekly*, December 29, 1995, p. 307.
3. Quoted in Kim Cunningham, "Comic Strip?" *People Weekly*, August 16, 1996, p. 108.

Chapter 1: Fitting In and Standing Out

4. Quoted in *British Premiere*, 1995. http://sandra.simplenet.com/sandra/bprem95.html.
5. Quoted in *British Premiere*.
6. Quoted in Jill Nelson, "Look at Me, I'm Sandra B.!" *McCall's StarStyle*, Fall 1999, p. 34.
7. Quoted in *British Premiere*.
8. Quoted in *Cosmopolitan*, 1994. http://sandra.simplenet.com/sandra/cosmo94.html.
9. Quoted in *British Premiere*.
10. Quoted in *British Premiere*.
11. Quoted in *British Premiere*.
12. Quoted in *British Premiere*.
13. Quoted in *People Weekly*, "50 Most Beautiful People," May 10, 1999, p. 199.
14. Quoted in Rebecca Ascher-Walsh, "No. 1 with a Bullock," *Entertainment Weekly*, May 5, 1995, p. 22.
15. Quoted in *British Vogue*, 1996. http://sandra.simplenet.com/

sandra/bvogue96.html.

16. Quoted in *US Magazine*, 1997. http://sandra.simplenet.com/sandra/usmag97.html.

17. Quoted in *British Vogue*.

18. Quoted in *British Vogue*.

19. Quoted in *British Vogue*.

20. Quoted in Cerio, "Speeding Bullock," p. 63.

21. Quoted in *Rolling Stone*, 1997. http://sandra.simplenet.com/sandra/rollingstone.html.

22. Quoted in *British Premiere*.

Chapter 2: Bit Parts

23. Quoted in *British Premiere*.

24. Quoted in *British Premiere*.

25. Quoted in Cerio, "Speeding Bullock," p. 64.

26. Quoted in *British Premiere*.

27. Quoted in *British Premiere*.

28. Quoted in Cerio, "Speeding Bullock," p. 65.

29. Quoted in *British Premiere*.

30. Quoted in Cerio, "Speeding Bullock," p. 65.

31. Quoted in *British Premiere*.

32. Quoted in *Vanity Fair*, 1995. http://sandra.simplenet.com/sandra/vanity95.html.

33. Quoted in Ascher-Walsh, "No. 1 with a Bullock," p. 23.

34. Quoted in Barry Koltnow, "Hollywood's Hottest Actress, Sandra Bullock, Tries to Fight Off Fame," Knight-Ridder/Tribune News Service, July 31, 1995.

35. Quoted in Koltnow, "Hollywood's Hottest Actress, Sandra Bullock, Tries to Fight Off Fame."

36. Quoted in David Rensin, "Sandra Bullock," *Playboy*, September 1995, p. 146.

Chapter 3: *Speeding* Ahead

37. Quoted in Luaine Lee, "'While You Were Sleeping' Star Is on the Fast Track to Fame," Knight-Ridder/Tribune News Service, April 17, 1995, p. 41.

38. Quoted in Ascher-Walsh, "No. 1 with a Bullock," p. 24.

39. Quoted in Frank Bruni, "'While You Were Sleeping' Star Bullock's Career Moves Full-Speed Ahead," Knight-Ridder/Tribune News Service, April 20, 1995, p. 42.
40. Quoted in *Vanity Fair.*
41. Quoted in Lee, "'While You Were Sleeping' Star Is on the Fast Track to Fame."
42. Quoted in *Rolling Stone.*
43. Quoted in *Rolling Stone.*
44. Quoted in *Rolling Stone.*
45. Quoted in *British Premiere.*
46. Quoted in *Rolling Stone.*
47. Quoted in Cerio, "Speeding Bullock," p. 65.
48. Bruce Fretts, "Love Potion #9," *Entertainment Weekly*, October 6, 1995, pp. 70–71.
49. Quoted in Lee, "'While You Were Sleeping' Star Is on the Fast Track to Fame."
50. Quoted in Ascher-Walsh, "No. 1 with a Bullock," p. 20.
51. Quoted in Koltnow, "Hollywood's Hottest Actress, Sandra Bullock, Tries to Fight off Fame."
52. Quoted in Koltnow, "Hollywood's Hottest Actress, Sandra Bullock, Tries to Fight off Fame."

Chapter 4: Professional Success/Personal Unhappiness

53. Quoted in Bruni, "'While You Were Sleeping' Star Bullock's Career Moves Full-Speed Ahead."
54. Quoted in Bruni, "'While You Were Sleeping' Star Bullock's Career Moves Full-Speed Ahead."
55. Quoted in Kim Cunningham, "While You Were Sanding," *People Weekly*, May 15, 1995, p. 146.
56. *E!Online*, "Q&A with Sandra Bullock," 1999. www.eonline.com/Celebs/Qa/Bullock99/interview2.html.
57. Quoted in Ascher-Walsh, "No. 1 with a Bullock," p. 22.
58. Quoted in Ascher-Walsh, "No. 1 with a Bullock," p. 21.
59. Quoted in Bruni, "'While You Were Sleeping' Star Bullock's Career Moves Full-Speed Ahead."
60. Quoted in Bruni, "'While You Were Sleeping' Star Bullock's

Career Moves Full-Speed Ahead."

61. Quoted in Koltnow, "Hollywood's Hottest Actress, Sandra Bullock, Tries to Fight Off Fame."

62. Quoted in Cerio, "Speeding Bullock," p. 64.

63. Quoted in Koltnow, "Hollywood's Hottest Actress, Sandra Bullock, Tries to Fight Off Fame."

64. Quoted in *People Weekly,* "Family Business," April 29, 1996, p. 20.

Chapter 5: New Roles

65. Quoted in Belinda Luscombe, "Now, Sandra Also Rises," *Time,* August 19, 1996, p. 75.

66. Quoted in Jean Oppenheimer, "Never Mind the Sex Pistols, Here Comes Sandra Bullock," *Mr. Showbiz,* 1996. http://mrshowbiz.go.com/interviews/246_1.html.

67. Quoted in Kim Cunningham, "That Thing You Do," *People Weekly,* January 27, 1997, p. 122.

68. Quoted in Oppenheimer, "Never Mind the Sex Pistols, Here Comes Sandra Bullock."

69. Quoted in Oppenheimer, "Never Mind the Sex Pistols, Here Comes Sandra Bullock."

70. Quoted in Leah Rozen, "Two If by Sea," *People Weekly,* January 29, 1996, p. 17.

71. Quoted in *Rolling Stone.*

72. Quoted in Oppenheimer, "Never Mind the Sex Pistols, Here Comes Sandra Bullock."

73. Quoted in Zoe Heller, "Two for the Road," *Harper's Bazaar,* April 1999, p. 164.

74. Quoted in *People Weekly,* "And Speaking for Miriam . . . ," December 21, 1998, p. 150.

75. Quoted in *People Weekly,* "And Speaking for Miriam . . . ," p. 150.

76. Quoted in *InStyle,* "The Lone Star Affair," May 1998, p. 232.

77. Quoted in Lee, "'While You Were Sleeping' Star Is on the Fast Track to Fame."

78. Quoted in *Rolling Stone.*

79. Quoted in Koltnow, "Hollywood's Hottest Actress, Sandra Bullock, Tries to Fight Off Fame."

Chapter 6: Sandra Style

80. Quoted in *Elle*, 1995. http://sandra.simplenet.com/sandra/elle95.html.
81. Quoted in *Elle*.
82. Quoted in Chuck Arnold, "Saying It Ain't So," *People Weekly*, June 30, 1997, p. 130.
83. Quoted in "Buds Lite: Matthew McConaughey and Sandra Bullock Swear They're Just Pals," *People Weekly*, February 24, 1997, p. 138.
84. Quoted in Holly Millea, "The Secret Life of Sandra Bullock," *Premiere*, April 2000, p. 74.
85. Quoted in *People Weekly*, "50 Most Beautiful People," May 10, 1999, p. 199.
86. Quoted in *People Weekly*, "50 Most Beautiful People," May 10, 1999, p. 199.
87. Quoted in *People Weekly*, "Sandra Bullock," p. 199
88. Quoted in *Playboy*, "Sandra Bullock," p. 148.
89. Quoted in *People Weekly*, "50 Most Beautiful People," May 10, 1999, p. 199.
90. Quoted in *Entertainment Weekly*, "Sandra Bullock," May 19, 1995, p. 55.
91. Quoted in Millea, "The Secret Life of Sandra Bullock," p. 106.

Chapter 7: Practically Magic

92. *Entertainment Weekly*, "Hex Education," October 23, 1998, p. 47.
93. Quoted in *People Weekly*, "Under Her Spell," October 19, 1998, p. 182.
94. Quoted in Heller, "Two for the Road," p. 184.
95. Quoted in Heller, "Two for the Road," p. 184.
96. Quoted in Heller, "Two for the Road," p. 184.
97. *E!Online*, "Q&A with Sandra Bullock," 1999.
98. *E!Online*, "Q&A with Sandra Bullock," 1999.
99. *Mr. Showbiz* review, "*Gun Shy*," February 4, 2000. http://mrshowbiz.go.com/reviews/moviereviews/movies/GunShy_2000.html.

100. Quoted in Lee, "'While You Were Sleeping' Star Is on the Fast Track to Fame."

101. Quoted in Millea, "The Secret Life of Sandra Bullock," p. 74.

102. Quoted in Millea, "The Secret Life of Sandra Bullock," p. 74.

103. *E!Online,* "Q&A with Sandra Bullock," 1999.

104. Quoted in *Entertainment Weekly,* "Sandra Bullock," December 29, 1995, p. 22.

Important Dates in the Life of Sandra Bullock

1964
Sandra Annette Bullock is born July 26 to John and Helga Bullock; she lives in Virginia and Germany until age 12.

1972
Performs onstage in German operas and decides to become an actress.

1976
Bullock family takes up permanent residence in Arlington, Virginia.

1982
Graduates from high school and attends East Carolina University.

1986
Drops out of East Carolina and moves to New York to begin an acting career; takes up bartending to pay the bills and attends acting classes.

1988
Stars in off-Broadway play *No Time Flat* and lands an agent.

1989
Moves to Los Angeles; lands roles in television movies *The Preppie Murder* and *Bionic Showdown: The Six Million Dollar Man and the Bionic Woman*.

1990
Stars in the television series *Working Girl*.

1991

Stars in *Love Potion No. 9.*

1994

Gets big break in blockbuster *Speed;* forms own production company, Fortis Films.

1995

Receives MTV Movie Awards for Best Female Performance in a Movie, Best On-screen Duo (with Keanu Reeves), and Most Desirable Female, and is awarded the Golden Apple Award for Female Star of the Year, and the NATO/ShoWest Award for Female Star of the Year.

1996

Commands more than $10 million for her role in *In Love and War.*

1997

Directs and stars in short film *Making Sandwiches.*

1998

Produces *Hope Floats.*

1999

Wins People's Choice Award for Favorite Motion Picture Actress; signs deal with Warner Brothers to produce two live-action and two animated films.

2000

Stars in *28 Days,* a film about an alcoholic going through rehabilitation.

For Further Reading

Rebecca Ascher-Walsh, "No. 1 with a Bullock," *Entertainment Weekly*, May 5, 1995.

———, "Sandra Bullock," *Entertainment Weekly*, December 29, 1995.

Gregory Cerio, "Speeding Bullock," *People Weekly*, August 14, 1995.

Holly Millea, "The Secret Life of Sandra Bullock," *Premiere*, April 2000.

Jill Nelson, "Look at Me, I'm Sandra B.!" *McCall's StarStyle*, Fall 1999.

Works Consulted

Periodicals

Chuck Arnold, "Saying It Ain't So," *People Weekly*, June 30, 1997.

Frank Bruni, "'While You Were Sleeping' Star Bullock's Career Moves Full-Speed Ahead," Knight-Ridder/Tribune News Service, April 20, 1995.

Kim Cunningham, "Comic Strip?" *People Weekly*, August 16, 1996.

———, "That Thing You Do," *People Weekly*, January 27, 1997.

———, "When She's Not Sleeping," *People Weekly*, July 31, 1995.

———, "While You Were Sanding," *People Weekly*, May 15, 1995.

Entertainment Weekly, "Hex Education," October 23, 1998.

———, "Sandra Bullock," May 19, 1995.

Rory Evans, "Speeding Bullock," *Allure*, April 2000.

Bruce Fretts, "Love Potion #9," *Entertainment Weekly*, October 6, 1995.

Zoe Heller, "Two for the Road," *Harper's Bazaar*, April 1999.

InStyle, "The Lone Star Affair," May 1998.

Barry Koltnow, "Hollywood's Hottest Actress, Sandra Bullock, Tries to Fight Off Fame," Knight-Ridder/Tribune News Service, July 31, 1995.

Luaine Lee, "'While You Were Sleeping' Star Is on the Fast Track to Fame," Knight-Ridder/Tribune News Service, April 17, 1995.

Belinda Luscombe, "Now, Sandra Also Rises," *Time*, August 19, 1996.

People Weekly, "And Speaking for Miriam . . . ," December 21, 1998.

———, "Buds Lite: Matthew McConaughey and Sandra Bullock Swear They're Just Pals," February 24, 1997.

———, "Family Business," April 29, 1996.

———, "50 Most Beautiful People," May 6, 1996.

———, "50 Most Beautiful People," May 10, 1999.

———, "Sailing On," June 15, 1998.

———, "Sandra Bullock," November 18, 1996.

———, "Under Her Spell," October 19, 1998.

David Rensin, "Sandra Bullock", *Playboy*, September 1995.

Leah Rozen, "Two If by Sea." *People Weekly*, January 29, 1996.

Internet Sources

British Premiere, 1995. http://sandra.simplenet.com/sandra/bprem
  95.html.

British Vogue, 1996. http://sandra.simplenet.com/sandra/bvogue96.
  html.

Cosmopolitan, 1994. http://sandra.simplenet.com/sandra/cosmo94.
  html.

Elle, 1995. http://sandra.simplenet.com/sandra/elle95.html.

E!Online, "Q&A with Sandra Bullock," 1996. www.eonline.com/
  Celebs/Qa/Bullock/interview2.html.

———, "Q&A with Sandra Bullock," 1999. www.eonline.com/
  Celebs/Qa/Bullock99/interview2.html.

Mr. Showbiz, "Bullock's a Babe with Car Crashes," September 10,
  1999.   http://mrshowbiz.go.com/archive/news/Todays_
  Stories/990910/bullock091099.html.

———, " *Gun Shy* review," February 4, 2000. http://mrshowbiz.
  go.com/reviews/moviereviews/movies/GunShy_2000.html.

Jean Oppenheimer, "Never Mind the Sex Pistols, Here Comes
  Sandra Bullock," *Mr. Showbiz*, 1996. http://mrshowbiz.go.
  com/interviews/246_1.html.

Rolling Stone, 1997.
  http://sandra.simplenet.com/sandra/rollingstone.html.

US Magazine, 1997.
  http://sandra.simplenet.com/sandra/usmag97.html.

Vanity Fair, 1995.
  http://sandra.simplenet.com/sandra/vanity95.html.

Websites

Belgium Sandra Bullock Page (http://sandra.simplenet.com/

sandra/idexf.htm). This website, containing pictures and many magazine articles about Bullock, can be accessed in both English and French.

Cyd's Too Cool Sandra Bullock Page (www.geocities.com/ Hollywood/6995/). Includes photos, quotes, sounds, links, and information about Sandra Bullock.

The Original Sandra Bullock Image Site (www.sandra.com). Features a filmography, current news, a biography, and many photos.

Index

Picture Credits

About the Author

Anne E. Hill has been writing for kids and teens since she was sixteen, and her first article was published in a teen magazine.

Now, ten years later, she is a freelance writer, editor, and the author of six books: *Denzel Washington,* which was named one of the New York Public Library's Best Books for Teenagers; *Ekaterina Gordeeva; Female Firsts in Their Fields: Broadcasting and Journalism; Cameron Diaz; Jennifer Lopez;* and *Sergei Grinkov.* Mrs. Hill is also a writer and voicer for the Concert Connection's All Star Teen Line.

Anne graduated Magna Cum Laude with a B.A. in English from Franklin and Marshall College, where she was a member of Phi Beta Kappa and wrote for the college's alumni magazine. She lives near Philadelphia with her husband, George. Her favorite Sandra Bullock film is *While You Were Sleeping.*